EASY CHOWI COOKBOOK

50 DELICIOUS CHOWDER RECIPES

By
BookSumo Press
Copyright © by Saxonberg Associates
All rights reserved

Published by
BookSumo Press, a DBA of Saxonberg Associates
http://www.booksumo.com/

ABOUT THE AUTHOR.

BookSumo Press is a publisher of unique, easy, and healthy cookbooks.

Our cookbooks span all topics and all subjects. If you want a deep dive into the possibilities of cooking with any type of ingredient. Then BookSumo Press is your go to place for robust yet simple and delicious cookbooks and recipes. Whether you are looking for great tasting pressure cooker recipes or authentic ethic and cultural food. BookSumo Press has a delicious and easy cookbook for you.

With simple ingredients, and even simpler step-by-step instructions BookSumo cookbooks get everyone in the kitchen chefing delicious meals.

BookSumo is an independent publisher of books operating in the beautiful Garden State (NJ) and our team of chefs and kitchen experts are here to teach, eat, and be merry!

INTRODUCTION

Welcome to *The Effortless Chef Series*! Thank you for taking the time to purchase this cookbook.

Come take a journey into the delights of easy cooking. The point of this cookbook and all BookSumo Press cookbooks is to exemplify the effortless nature of cooking simply.

In this book we focus on Chowder. You will find that even though the recipes are simple, the taste of the dishes are quite amazing.

So will you take an adventure in simple cooking? If the answer is yes please consult the table of contents to find the dishes you are most interested in.

Once you are ready, jump right in and start cooking.

— BookSumo Press

TABLE OF CONTENTS

About the Author 2

Introduction 3

Table of Contents 4

Any Issues? Contact Us 8

Legal Notes 9

Common Abbreviations 10

Chapter 1: Easy Chowder Recipes 11

    New England Salmon Chowder 11

    Louisiana Crawfish Chowder 14

    Shrimp, Calamari, Crab Chowder 17

    Maine Mushroom Cod Chowder 20

    American Ground Beef Chowder 23

    Meatless-Monday Chowder 25

    Newfoundland Cod Fillet Parsley Chowder 28

    Mexican Dinner Chowder 31

    Economical Macaroni Clam Chowder 34

Winter Night Chowder 36
February Shrimp Chowder 39
Rosa's Latin Chowder 41
Winter Country Leeks Chowder 44
Southwestern Chowder 47
Chowder Dump Dinner 50
Full Creole Corn Chowder 52
Clam Clásico 56
Summer Carnival Chowder 59
New Jersey Diner Inspired Chowder 62
Chicken Chowder for Champions 65
All About the Chowder 68
Maria's Potluck Chowder 70
Buttery Green Bean Chowder 73
Grocery Store Rotisserie Chowder 76
Condensed Cream Cheese Chowder 79
Milanese Chowder 81
60-Minute Corn Chowder 84
South Carolina Catfish Inspired Chowder 86
Utica Inspired Chowder 89

How to Make a Fresh Corn Chowder 92
Chowder 101 95
Country Roasted Chicken and Broccoli Chowder 98
Caribbean Conch and Corn Chowder 102
Saskatchewan Country Chowder 105
How to Make a Can of Chowder 108
Saturday's Dinner 110
Veggie Sampler Chowder 113
Rust Belt Chowder 116
Providence Inspired Chuckle Chowder 118
Chopped Chowder 121
San Pedro Pepper Jack Chowder 124
Georgia Mixed Veggie Chowder 127
Classic Canadian Chowder 130
Southern Parisian Chowder 133
November's Chowder 136
Staten Island Inspired Chowder 139
American Comfort Chowder 141
2-Cheese Red Potato Chowder 144
Leek Lunch Box Chowder 147

Sanibel Island Scallop Chowder 150

Lemon Pepper Seafood Sampler Chowder 153

THANKS FOR READING! JOIN THE CLUB AND KEEP ON COOKING WITH 6 MORE COOKBOOKS.... 156

Come On 158

Let's Be Friends :) 158

ANY ISSUES? CONTACT US

If you find that something important to you is missing from this book please contact us at info@booksumo.com.

We will take your concerns into consideration when the 2nd edition of this book is published. And we will keep you updated!

— BookSumo Press

LEGAL NOTES

ALL RIGHTS RESERVED. NO PART OF THIS BOOK MAY BE REPRODUCED OR TRANSMITTED IN ANY FORM OR BY ANY MEANS. PHOTOCOPYING, POSTING ONLINE, AND / OR DIGITAL COPYING IS STRICTLY PROHIBITED UNLESS WRITTEN PERMISSION IS GRANTED BY THE BOOK'S PUBLISHING COMPANY. LIMITED USE OF THE BOOK'S TEXT IS PERMITTED FOR USE IN REVIEWS WRITTEN FOR THE PUBLIC.

COMMON ABBREVIATIONS

cup(s)	C.
tablespoon	tbsp
teaspoon	tsp
ounce	oz.
pound	lb

*All units used are standard American measurements

Chapter 1: Easy Chowder Recipes

New England Salmon Chowder

Ingredients

- 3 tbsp butter
- 3/4 C. chopped onion
- 1/2 C. chopped celery
- 1 tsp garlic powder
- 2 C. diced potatoes
- 2 carrots, diced
- 2 C. chicken broth
- 1 tsp salt
- 1 tsp ground black pepper
- 1 tsp dried dill weed
- 2 (16 oz.) cans salmon
- 1 (12 fluid oz.) can evaporated milk
- 1 (15 oz.) can creamed corn
- 1/2 lb. Cheddar cheese, shredded

Directions

- In a large pan, melt the butter on medium heat and sauté the onion, celery and garlic powder till tender.

- Stir in the potatoes, carrots, broth, salt, pepper and dill and bring to a boil.
- Reduce the heat and simmer, covered for about 20 minutes.
- Stir in the salmon, evaporated milk, corn and cheese and cook till heated completely.

Amount per serving 8

Timing Information:

Preparation	15 m
Cooking	30 m
Total Time	45 m

Nutritional Information:

Calories	490 kcal
Fat	25.9 g
Carbohydrates	26.5g
Protein	38.6 g
Cholesterol	104 mg
Sodium	1140 mg

* Percent Daily Values are based on a 2,000 calorie diet.

Louisiana Crawfish Chowder

Ingredients

- 1/4 C. butter
- 1/2 bunch green onions, chopped
- 1/2 C. butter
- 2 lb. frozen crawfish, cleaned
- 2 (10.75 oz.) cans condensed cream of potato soup
- 1 (10.75 oz.) can condensed cream of mushroom soup
- 1 (15.25 oz.) can whole kernel corn, drained
- 4 oz. cream cheese, softened
- 2 C. half-and-half cream
- 1/2 tsp cayenne pepper

Directions

- In a pan, melt 1/4 C. of the butter on medium heat and sauté the green onions till tender.
- Transfer the green onions into a bowl and keep aside.
- In the same pan, melt 1/2 C. of the butter and sauté the crawfish for about 5 minutes.
- Remove from the heat and keep aside.
- In a large pan, mix together the potato soup, mushroom soup, corn and cream cheese on medium heat and bring to a gentle boil.

- Stir in the half-and-half, cooked green onions, crawfish and cayenne pepper and bring to a gentle boil.
- Simmer for about 5 minutes.

Amount per serving 10

Timing Information:

Preparation	20 m
Cooking	25 m
Total Time	45 m

Nutritional Information:

Calories	395 kcal
Fat	27.5 g
Carbohydrates	20.6g
Protein	17.7 g
Cholesterol	167 mg
Sodium	934 mg

* Percent Daily Values are based on a 2,000 calorie diet.

Shrimp, Calamari, Crab Chowder

Ingredients

- 1 1/2 C. fat free milk
- 1 (8 oz.) container fat free cream cheese
- 2 cloves garlic, minced
- 1 (26 oz.) can fat free condensed cream of mushroom soup
- 1 C. chopped green onions
- 1 C. sliced carrots
- 1 (15.25 oz.) can whole kernel corn, undrained
- 1 1/2 C. chopped potatoes
- 1 tsp dried parsley
- 1/2 tsp ground black pepper
- 1/2 tsp ground cayenne pepper
- 1/2 lb. shrimp
- 1/2 lb. bay scallops
- 1/2 lb. crabmeat
- 1/2 lb. calamari tubes
- 1 (6.5 oz.) can chopped clams

Directions

- In a large pan, add 1/2 C. of the milk, cream cheese and garlic on low heat and cook till well combined, stirring continuously.

- Stir in the soup, green onions, carrots, corn with liquid, potatoes, parsley, remaining milk, black pepper and cayenne pepper and simmer for about 25 minutes.
- Stir in the shrimp, scallops, crabmeat, calamari and clams and simmer for about 10 minutes.

Amount per serving 8

Timing Information:

Preparation	15 m
Cooking	45 m
Total Time	1 h

Nutritional Information:

Calories	314 kcal
Fat	5.1 g
Carbohydrates	32g
Protein	34.6 g
Cholesterol	158 mg
Sodium	1237 mg

* Percent Daily Values are based on a 2,000 calorie diet.

MAINE MUSHROOM COD CHOWDER

Ingredients

- 2 tbsp butter
- 2 C. chopped onion
- 4 fresh mushrooms, sliced
- 1 stalk celery, chopped
- 4 C. chicken stock
- 4 C. diced potatoes
- 2 lb. cod, diced into 1/2 inch cubes
- 1/8 tsp Old Bay Seasoning
- Salt to taste
- Ground black pepper to taste
- 1 C. clam juice
- 1/2 C. all-purpose flour
- 2 (12 fluid oz.) cans evaporated milk

Directions

- In a large pan, melt 2 tbsp of the butter on medium heat and sauté the onions, mushrooms and celery till tender.
- Add the chicken stock and potatoes and simmer for about 10 minutes.
- Add the fish and simmer for about 10 minutes.

- Stir in the Old Bay seasoning, salt, pepper, clam juice and flour and cook till smooth, stirring continuously.
- Remove from heat and immediately, stir in the evaporated milk.
- Serve hot.

Amount per serving 8

Timing Information:

Preparation	30 m
Cooking	30 m
Total Time	1 h

Nutritional Information:

Calories	356 kcal
Fat	11.3 g
Carbohydrates	33.7g
Protein	29.8 g
Cholesterol	77 mg
Sodium	618 mg

* Percent Daily Values are based on a 2,000 calorie diet.

AMERICAN GROUND BEEF CHOWDER

Ingredients

- 2 lb. ground beef
- 2 (15 oz.) cans diced new potatoes
- 1 C. chopped onion
- 4 C. milk
- 1 lb. processed cheese food, cut into chunks
- 1/2 lb. sharp Cheddar cheese, cut into chunks
- Ground black pepper to taste
- 2/3 C. mashed potatoes

Directions

- Heat a large pan on medium-high heat and cook the beef for about 5-7 minutes.
- Drain the excess grease from the pan.
- In the same pan, add the diced potatoes and onion and cook for about 5-10 minutes.
- Stir in the milk, processed cheese food and Cheddar cheese and bring to a boil.
- Reduce the heat and simmer for about 15-20 minutes, stirring occasionally.
- Stir in the pepper and mashed potatoes and cook for about 5 minutes.

Amount per serving 10

Timing Information:

Preparation	10 m
Cooking	35 m
Total Time	45 m

Nutritional Information:

Calories	540 kcal
Fat	34.9 g
Carbohydrates	21.6g
Protein	34.3 g
Cholesterol	117 mg
Sodium	912 mg

* Percent Daily Values are based on a 2,000 calorie diet.

Meatless-Monday Chowder

Ingredients

- 1/2 C. chopped red bell pepper
- 1/2 C. chopped onion
- 1/4 C. margarine
- 1 C. chopped celery
- 1 C. cauliflower, chopped
- 1 C. diced carrots
- 1 C. fresh chopped broccoli
- 3 C. water
- 3 cubes chicken bouillon
- 1/2 C. all-purpose flour
- 1 tbsp chopped fresh parsley
- 3 C. shredded Cheddar cheese
- Salt to taste
- Ground black pepper to taste
- 1 1/2 C. milk

Directions

- In a Dutch oven, melt the margarine and sauté the pepper and onions till tender.
- Add the remaining vegetables, water, bouillon, salt and pepper and bring to a boil.

- Reduce the heat and simmer, covered for about 20 minutes.
- In a bowl, add the flour and milk and mix till smooth.
- Add the flour mixture into the pan and stir to combine.
- Bring to a boil, stirring continuously.
- Cook for about 2 minutes, stirring continuously.
- Stir in the parsley and cheese and cook till the cheese melts completely.

Amount per serving 7

Timing Information:

Preparation	15 m
Cooking	35 m
Total Time	50 m

Nutritional Information:

Calories	341 kcal
Fat	23.9 g
Carbohydrates	16g
Protein	16.3 g
Cholesterol	55 mg
Sodium	927 mg

* Percent Daily Values are based on a 2,000 calorie diet.

Newfoundland Cod Fillet Parsley Chowder

Ingredients

- 8 slices bacon, diced
- 1 large onion, diced
- 1 red bell pepper, seeded and diced
- Salt and ground black pepper to taste
- 2 cloves garlic, chopped
- 1 1/2 tbsp seafood seasoning
- 1 (16 oz.) can chicken broth
- 3 red potatoes cut into 1/2-inch cubes
- 4 ears sweet corn, shucked and kernels cut off
- 1/2 C. water
- 2 C. whole milk
- 2 tbsp butter
- 1 lb. thick cod fillets, cut into 1-inch pieces
- 2 tbsp chopped fresh flat-leaf parsley

Directions

- Heat a large pan on medium heat and cook the bacon for about 10 minutes.

- Transfer the bacon onto a paper towel lined plate to drain, leaving the grease in the pan.
- In the same pan, sauté the onion and red bell pepper for about 5 minutes.
- Stir in the salt, pepper, garlic and seafood seasoning and sauté for about 2 minutes.
- Stir in the chicken broth, water, potatoes and corn and bring to a boil.
- Reduce the heat to low and simmer for about 15 minutes.
- Stir in the milk and butter and simmer till the butter melts.
- Stir in the reserved bacon and bring to a gentle boil.
- Stir in the cod and parsley and cook for 5-8 minutes, stirring occasionally.

Amount per serving 6

Timing Information:

Preparation	20 m
Cooking	40 m
Total Time	1 h

Nutritional Information:

Calories	408 kcal
Fat	24.9 g
Carbohydrates	23.1g
Protein	23.8 g
Cholesterol	78 mg
Sodium	1206 mg

* Percent Daily Values are based on a 2,000 calorie diet.

Mexican Dinner Chowder

Ingredients

- 2/3 C. chopped onion
- 1/2 C. chopped red bell pepper
- 1/3 C. chopped green chili pepper
- 2 tbsp minced garlic
- 1 jalapeño pepper, seeded and diced
- 1 tbsp margarine
- 3 C. vegetable broth
- 2 C. peeled and cubed potatoes
- 1 tsp ground cumin
- 1/2 tsp salt
- 1/8 tsp ground black pepper
- 1/8 tsp ground red pepper
- 2 C. cheese tortellini
- 2 tbsp all-purpose flour
- 2 tbsp vegetable oil
- 1 (15 oz.) can whole kernel corn, drained
- 1 pint half-and-half cream

Directions

- In a large pan, melt the margarine on medium heat and sauté the onion, bell pepper, chili pepper, garlic and jalapeño pepper for about 5 minutes.
- Stir in the broth, potatoes, cumin, salt, pepper and red pepper and bring to a boil.
- Reduce the heat to low and simmer for about 20 minutes.
- Meanwhile in a large pan of the lightly salted boiling water, cook the pasta for about 8-10 minutes.
- Drain well and keep aside.
- In a small bowl, mix together the flour and vegetable oil.
- Add the oil mixture into the soup and stir to combine.
- Increase the heat to medium and cook till the mixture becomes thick and bubbly.
- Stir in the corn, half-and-half and tortellini and cook till heated completely.
- Serve hot.

Amount per serving 8

Timing Information:

Preparation	15 m
Cooking	40 m
Total Time	55 m

Nutritional Information:

Calories	322 kcal
Fat	16 g
Carbohydrates	38.8g
Protein	8.9 g
Cholesterol	38 mg
Sodium	622 mg

* Percent Daily Values are based on a 2,000 calorie diet.

Economical Macaroni Clam Chowder

Ingredients

- 3 quarts water
- 3 tbsp salt
- 2 C. elbow macaroni
- 2 (6.5 oz.) cans minced clams
- 2 C. chopped tomatoes
- 1 (4 oz.) can chopped green chili peppers
- 1 (14.5 oz.) can chicken broth
- 1/2 C. shredded Cheddar cheese

Directions

- In a large pan of the lightly salted boiling water, cook the macaroni till tender.
- Drain the macaroni and return to the pan.
- Add the clams, tomatoes, chili peppers and chicken broth and toss to coat and gently warm.
- Serve with a topping of the grated cheese.

Amount per serving 4

Timing Information:

Preparation	15 m
Cooking	40 m
Total Time	55 m

Nutritional Information:

Calories	410 kcal
Fat	7.5 g
Carbohydrates	49.1g
Protein	35 g
Cholesterol	77 mg
Sodium	5781 mg

* Percent Daily Values are based on a 2,000 calorie diet.

Winter Night Chowder

Ingredients

- 2 tbsp unsalted butter
- 1 yellow onion, finely chopped
- 4 stalks celery, cut into 1/4-inch slices
- 1 tbsp finely chopped fresh thyme
- Salt and ground black pepper to taste
- 7 potatoes cut into 1/2-inch pieces
- 2 C. whole milk
- 1 (15 oz.) can fish broth
- 1 C. heavy whipping cream
- 1 (8 oz.) bottle clam juice
- 1 1/2 lb. Dungeness crab meat, chopped

Directions

- In a large pan, melt the butter on medium heat and sauté the onion, celery, thyme, salt and pepper for about 5 minutes.
- Stir in the potatoes, milk, broth, cream, and clam juice and bring to a gentle boil.
- Cook for about 10 minutes.
- Remove from the heat and keep aside to cool slightly.

- In a blender, add the broth mixture in batches and pulse till smooth.
- Return the pureed soup to the pan and stir in the crab meat.
- Cook for about 5 minutes.
- Stir in the salt and pepper and remove from the heat.

Amount per serving 6

Timing Information:

Preparation	20 m
Cooking	20 m
Total Time	40 m

Nutritional Information:

Calories	560 kcal
Fat	23.3 g
Carbohydrates	52.2g
Protein	35.8 g
Cholesterol	160 mg
Sodium	883 mg

* Percent Daily Values are based on a 2,000 calorie diet.

FEBRUARY SHRIMP CHOWDER

Ingredients

- 1/2 C. sliced celery
- 1/3 C. finely diced onion
- 2 tbsp margarine
- 1 (8 oz.) package cream cheese, diced
- 1 C. milk
- 1 1/2 C. cubed potatoes
- 1/2 lb. frozen cooked shrimp, thawed and drained
- 2 tbsp dry white wine
- 1/2 tsp salt

Directions

- In a large stock pot sauté celery and onions in margarine
- Add cream cheese and milk; and stir over low heat until cream cheese is completely melted.
- Add potatoes, shrimp, dry white wine and salt. Heat thorough, stirring occasionally and then serve.

Amount per serving 4

Timing Information:

Preparation	20 m
Cooking	20 m
Total Time	40 m

Nutritional Information:

Calories	400 kcal
Fat	27.1 g
Carbohydrates	16.4g
Protein	21.9 g
Cholesterol	181 mg
Sodium	722 mg

* Percent Daily Values are based on a 2,000 calorie diet.

Rosa's Latin Chowder

Ingredients

- 1 1/2 lb. boneless skinless chicken breasts cut into bite-size pieces
- 1/2 C. chopped onion
- 1 clove garlic, minced
- 3 tbsp butter
- 2 cubes chicken bouillon
- 1 C. hot water
- 3/4 tsp ground cumin
- 2 C. half-and-half cream
- 2 C. shredded Monterey Jack cheese
- 1 (14.75 oz.) can cream-style corn
- 1 (4 oz.) can diced green chilis
- 1 dash hot pepper sauce
- 1 tomato, chopped
- Fresh cilantro sprigs, for garnish

Directions

- In a Dutch oven, melt the butter on medium heat and cook the chicken, onion and garlic till the chicken is no longer pink.
- In a bowl, dissolve the bouillon in hot water.

- Add the bouillon mixture into the Dutch oven and stir to combine.
- Stir in the cumin and bring to a boil.
- Reduce the heat to low and simmer, covered for about 5 minutes.
- Stir in the cream, cheese, corn, chilies and hot pepper sauce and simmer till the cheese is melted, stirring occasionally.
- Stir in the chopped tomato and remove from the heat.
- Serve with a garnishing of the cilantro.

Amount per serving 8

Timing Information:

Preparation	20 m
Cooking	35 m
Total Time	55 m

Nutritional Information:

Calories	367 kcal
Fat	21.3 g
Carbohydrates	15.1g
Protein	30 g
Cholesterol	109 mg
Sodium	868 mg

* Percent Daily Values are based on a 2,000 calorie diet.

Winter Country Leeks Chowder

Ingredients

- 8 C. chicken
- 4 C. cubed Country ham, optional
- 4 tbsp dried rosemary
- 2 lb turkey. bacon, diced
- 2 large onions, diced
- 3 leeks, diced
- 3 cloves garlic, minced
- 6 green onions, diced
- 6 large potatoes, cubed
- 1 lb. carrots, cubed
- 1 1/2 C. heavy cream

Directions

- In a large pan, add the stock on medium heat and bring to a boil.
- Stir in the cubed ham and 2 tbsp of the rosemary.
- Heat a large skillet on medium heat and cook the diced bacon till crisp.
- Transfer the bacon into the pan of simmering ham mixture.
- Drain the bacon grease, leaving 1/2 of in the skillet.

- Place the skillet on medium heat and sauté the onions, leeks, garlic and green onions till tender.
- Transfer the leek mixture into the pan of simmering ham mixture.
- Stir in the cubed potatoes, carrots and 2 tbsp of the rosemary and simmer for about 20 minutes.
- Remove from the heat and top with the cream.

Amount per serving 15

Timing Information:

Preparation	40 m
Cooking	40 m
Total Time	1 h 20 m

Nutritional Information:

Calories	438 kcal
Fat	24.8 g
Carbohydrates	35.8g
Protein	19.1 g
Cholesterol	76 mg
Sodium	1351 mg

* Percent Daily Values are based on a 2,000 calorie diet.

Southwestern Chowder

Ingredients

- 2 tbsp margarine
- 1 C. chopped celery
- 1 C. chopped onion
- 2 (14.5 oz.) cans chicken broth
- 3 C. peeled and cubed potatoes
- 1 (15 oz.) can whole kernel corn
- 1 (4 oz.) can diced green chilis
- 1 (2.5 oz.) package country style gravy mix
- 2 C. milk
- 1 C. shredded Mexican-style processed cheese food

Directions

- In a large pan, melt the margarine on medium-high heat and sauté the celery and onion for about 5 minutes.
- Add the chicken broth and bring to a boil.
- Stir in the potatoes.
- Reduce the heat to low and simmer for about 20-25 minutes, stirring occasionally.
- Stir in the corn and chilis and bring to a simmer.
- In a bowl, dissolve the gravy mix in milk.

- Add the gravy mixture into the boiling mixture and stir to combine.
- Add the cheese and cook till the cheese melts completely.

Amount per serving 7

Timing Information:

Preparation	20 m
Cooking	35 m
Total Time	55 m

Nutritional Information:

Calories	289 kcal
Fat	11.8 g
Carbohydrates	37.8g
Protein	11.3 g
Cholesterol	23 mg
Sodium	1021 mg

* Percent Daily Values are based on a 2,000 calorie diet.

Chowder Dump Dinner

Ingredients

- 1 (10.75 oz.) can condensed cream of celery soup
- 1 (10.75 oz.) can condensed cream of potato soup
- 1 (10.75 oz.) can New England clam chowder
- 2 (6.5 oz.) cans minced clams
- 1 quart half-and-half cream
- 1 pint heavy whipping cream

Directions

- In a slow cooker, mix together all
- Ingredients set the slow cooker on Low and cook, covered for about 6-8 hours.

Amount per serving 10

Timing Information:

Preparation	10 m
Cooking	8 h
Total Time	8 h 10 m

Nutritional Information:

Calories	425 kcal
Fat	32.5 g
Carbohydrates	17.6g
Protein	16.1 g
Cholesterol	134 mg
Sodium	740 mg

* Percent Daily Values are based on a 2,000 calorie diet.

Full Creole Corn Chowder

Ingredients

- 5 slices bacon
- 1 tbsp clarified butter
- 3/4 C. chopped onion
- 1/4 C. chopped green bell pepper
- 1/2 C. chopped celery
- 1 1/2 tsp minced garlic
- 1/4 C. dry white wine
- 1 tsp brandy
- 1 1/2 tsp dried basil
- 1 tsp ground white pepper
- 1/4 tsp cayenne pepper
- 1/2 tsp dried thyme leaves
- 2 tsp Worcestershire sauce
- 3 C. fresh corn kernels
- 4 large potatoes, peeled and diced
- 1 1/2 quarts chicken stock
- 1/2 C. butter
- 1/2 C. all-purpose flour
- 3 C. heavy cream
- 1 C. half-and-half cream
- 1 lb. peeled and deveined small shrimp
- 1 tbsp Creole seasoning

- 1 lb. fresh lump crabmeat, shell pieces removed

Directions

- Heat a large skillet on medium-high heat and cook the bacon for about 10 minutes, stirring occasionally.
- Transfer the bacon onto a paper towel lined plate to drain and then crumble it.
- Drain the grease from the skillet and reserve in a bowl.
- Meanwhile in a large pan, melt 1 tbsp of clarified butter on medium heat and cook the onion, green pepper, celery and garlic for about 10 minutes.
- Stir in the white wine and brandy and bring to a gentle boil.
- Stir in the basil, white pepper, cayenne pepper, thyme, Worcestershire sauce, corn, potatoes and chicken stock and bring to a boil on high heat.
- Reduce the heat to medium-low and simmer, covered for about 10 minutes.
- Meanwhile in a small pan, melt 1/2 C. of the butter on medium-low heat.
- Stir in the flour and cook for about 10 minutes, stirring continuously.
- Add the roux into the soup and stir to combine.
- Increase the heat to medium-high.
- Stir in the heavy cream, half-and-half cream, shrimp, reserved bacon and grease and cook for about 15 minutes.

- Stir in the Creole seasoning and crab meat and serve immediately.

Amount per serving 10

Timing Information:

Preparation	35 m
Cooking	40 m
Total Time	1 h 15 m

Nutritional Information:

Calories	709 kcal
Fat	48 g
Carbohydrates	46.1g
Protein	25.1 g
Cholesterol	240 mg
Sodium	1016 mg

* Percent Daily Values are based on a 2,000 calorie diet.

Clam Clásico

Ingredients

- 1/2 C. butter
- 1 1/2 large onions, chopped
- 3/4 C. all-purpose flour
- 1 quart shucked clams, with liquid
- 6 (8 oz.) jars clam juice
- 1 lb. boiling potatoes, peeled and chopped
- 3 C. half-and-half cream
- Salt and pepper to taste
- 1/2 tsp chopped fresh dill weed

Directions

- In a large pan, melt the butter on medium heat and sauté the onions till translucent.
- Reduce the heat to low.
- Stir in the flour and cook for about 2-4 minutes, stirring occasionally.
- Remove from the heat and keep aside to cool.
- In another pan, add the clams and clam juice and bring to a boil.
- Reduce the heat and simmer for about 15 minutes.

- In a small pan, add the peeled potatoes and enough water to cover and bring to a boil.
- Cook for about 15 minutes.
- Drain the potatoes and keep aside.
- Place the pan of flour mixture on medium heat.
- Slowly, add the hot clam stock into flour mixture, stirring continuously.
- Bring to a boil, stirring continuously.
- Reduce the heat and stir in the cooked potatoes.
- Stir in the half and half, salt and pepper and chopped dill and cook till heated completely.

Amount per serving 8

Timing Information:

Preparation	30 m
Cooking	30 m
Total Time	1 h

Nutritional Information:

Calories	337 kcal
Fat	22.4 g
Carbohydrates	25.8g
Protein	9.1 g
Cholesterol	78 mg
Sodium	627 mg

* Percent Daily Values are based on a 2,000 calorie diet.

Summer Carnival Chowder

Ingredients

- 1 tbsp unsalted butter
- 1 large onion, finely diced
- 2 large potatoes, peeled and cubed
- 2 cloves garlic, minced
- 6 C. chicken stock
- 1 (8 oz.) can stewed tomatoes, diced
- 2 large carrots, shredded
- 1 1/2 C. milk
- 1/2 C. heavy cream
- Salt and pepper to taste
- 2 lb. halibut, cut into 1-inch cubes
- 1/2 C. shredded Cheddar cheese
- 1 pinch red pepper flakes

Directions

- In a large pan, melt the butter on medium heat and sauté the onion for about 5 minutes.
- Add the potatoes and garlic and cook for about 10 minutes.
- Add the chicken stock, tomatoes and carrots and bring to a boil.

- Reduce the heat to medium-low and simmer, covered for about 10 minutes.
- Add the milk, cream, salt, pepper and halibut and simmer, uncovered for about 10 minutes.
- Gently stir in the Cheddar cheese and red pepper flakes till the cheese melts completely.
- Serve immediately.

Amount per serving 16

Timing Information:

Preparation	35 m
Cooking	40 m
Total Time	1 h 15 m

Nutritional Information:

Calories	172 kcal
Fat	6.5 g
Carbohydrates	12.5g
Protein	15.4 g
Cholesterol	39 mg
Sodium	364 mg

* Percent Daily Values are based on a 2,000 calorie diet.

New Jersey Diner Inspired Chowder

Ingredients

- 2 tbsp butter
- 1 tbsp olive oil
- 1 C. chopped onion
- 2 cloves garlic, chopped
- 1/2 C. chopped celery
- 1/2 C. all-purpose flour
- 6 C. chicken broth
- 1 lb. potatoes - peeled and cubed
- 1 tsp dried dill weed
- 1 tsp dried tarragon
- 1 tsp dried thyme
- 1/2 tsp paprika
- 8 oz. smoked salmon, cut into 1/2 inch pieces
- 1/4 C. white wine
- 1 tbsp fresh lemon juice
- 1/4 tsp hot sauce
- 1 tsp salt
- 1 tsp fresh-ground black pepper
- 1 C. half and half

Directions

- In a large span, mix together the butter, olive oil, onion, garlic and celery on medium-high heat and cook for 8-10 minutes.
- Add the flour and stir to combine well.
- Slowly, add the chicken broth and stir till mixture becomes slightly thick.
- Stir in the potatoes, dill, tarragon, thyme and paprika.
- Reduce the heat to medium and simmer, covered for about 15 minutes.
- Stir in the salmon, wine, lemon juice, hot sauce, salt and pepper.
- Reduce the heat to low and simmer, uncovered for about 10 minutes.
- Stir in the half-and-half and simmer for about 30 minutes, stirring occasionally.
- Serve hot.

Amount per serving 8

Timing Information:

Preparation	35 m
Cooking	1 h 5 m
Total Time	1 h 40 m

Nutritional Information:

Calories	205 kcal
Fat	9.5 g
Carbohydrates	20.5g
Protein	8.5 g
Cholesterol	25 mg
Sodium	561 mg

* Percent Daily Values are based on a 2,000 calorie diet.

Chicken Chowder for Champions

Ingredients

- 4 C. chicken broth
- 1 1/2 C. diced potatoes
- 1 C. diced celery
- 1 C. diced carrots
- 1 C. diced onion
- 1/3 C. margarine
- 1/3 C. all-purpose flour
- 3 C. milk
- 1 tbsp soy sauce
- 1 lb. processed cheese, cubed
- 2 C. chopped, cooked chicken meat

Directions

- In a large pan, mix together the chicken broth, potatoes, celery, carrots and onion and cook, covered for about 15 minutes.
- In a medium pan, melt the butter on low heat.
- Stir in the flour and cook for about 1 minute, stirring continuously.
- Slowly, add the milk, beating continuously.

- Cook till the mixture becomes thick and bubbly, stirring continuously.
- Add the flour mixture and soy sauce into the vegetables and stir to combine.
- Stir in the cheese till melts completely.
- Stir in the chicken and cook till heated completely.

Amount per serving 5

Timing Information:

Preparation	20m
Cooking	30m
Total Time	50m

Nutritional Information:

Calories	691 kcal
Fat	41.3 g
Carbohydrates	35.7g
Protein	43.5 g
Cholesterol	126 mg
Sodium	2209 mg

* Percent Daily Values are based on a 2,000 calorie diet.

All About the Chowder

Ingredients

- 6 C. peeled and cubed potatoes
- 1 tsp salt
- 1/2 tsp dried marjoram
- 3 C. water
- 1 lb. sausage, optional
- 1 onion, chopped
- 1 (15.25 oz.) can whole kernel corn
- 1 (14.75 oz.) can creamed corn
- 1 (12 fluid oz.) can evaporated milk

Directions

- In a large pan, add the potatoes, salt, marjoram and water and bring to a boil.
- Boil till the potatoes become just tender.
- Heat a skillet on medium heat and cook the sausage till browned completely.
- Drain off the excess grease from the skillet.
- Add the sausage into the potatoes and stir to combine.
- Stir in the cans of corn and the evaporated milk and cook till heat completely.
- Serve immediately.

Amount per serving 6

Timing Information:

Preparation	15 m
Cooking	30 m
Total Time	45 m

Nutritional Information:

Calories	634 kcal
Fat	36.4 g
Carbohydrates	61.7g
Protein	19.5 g
Cholesterol	70 mg
Sodium	1377 mg

* Percent Daily Values are based on a 2,000 calorie diet.

Maria's Potluck Chowder

Ingredients

- 10 slices turkey bacon, chopped
- 2 large onions, finely chopped
- 4 stalks celery, finely chopped
- 3 carrots, finely chopped
- 5 green onions, finely chopped
- 1/3 C. chopped fresh parsley
- 1/2 C. water
- 6 C. fish stock
- Salt to taste
- 1 1/2 tbsp ground black pepper
- 1 1/2 tbsp dried dill weed
- 8 red potatoes, cubed
- 1 C. butter
- 1 C. all-purpose flour
- 5 C. milk
- 3/4 C. white wine
- 1/4 C. lemon juice
- 1 1/2 lb. flaked or chopped smoked salmon
- 1 1/2 C. frozen corn kernels

Directions

- Heat a large pan on medium heat and cook the bacon for a few minutes to release some of the drippings.
- Add the onions and celery and sauté till tender.
- Stir in the carrots, green onions, parsley, water, fish stock, salt, pepper and dill.
- Reduce the heat to low and simmer, covered for about 15 minutes.
- Stir in the potatoes and simmer for about 20 minutes.
- Meanwhile in a small skillet, melt the butter on medium heat.
- Stir in the flour and cook till smooth and light brown, stirring continuously.
- Slowly, add the milk, a little bit at a time of the milk, beating continuously.
- Add the roux and remaining milk into the pan with the vegetables and cook till heated completely, stirring continuously.
- Stir in the white wine, lemon juice, smoked salmon and corn and cook till heated completely.
- Serve immediately.

Amount per serving 6

Timing Information:

Preparation	20 m
Cooking	1 h
Total Time	1 h 20 m

Nutritional Information:

Calories	1144 kcal
Fat	63.3 g
Carbohydrates	93.1g
Protein	48.4 g
Cholesterol	155 mg
Sodium	2405 mg

* Percent Daily Values are based on a 2,000 calorie diet.

Buttery Green Bean Chowder

Ingredients

- 7 C. water
- 9 cubes chicken bouillon, crumbled
- 6 potatoes, cubed
- 2 cloves garlic, minced
- 1 large white onion, chopped
- 1 bunch celery, chopped
- 3 C. chopped carrots
- 2 (15 oz.) cans whole kernel corn
- 2 (15 oz.) cans peas
- 2 C. chopped fresh green beans
- 1/2 C. butter
- 1/2 C. all-purpose flour
- 3 C. milk
- 1 lb. processed cheese, cubed

Directions

- In a large pan, mix together the water, bouillon, potatoes and garlic on medium heat and bring to a boil.
- Stir in the onion, celery and carrots.
- Reduce the heat to low and simmer for about 15 minutes.

- Stir in the corn, peas and green beans and cook on low heat.
- Meanwhile for the roux, in a medium pan, melt the butter on medium heat.
- Stir in the flour and cook for about 10 seconds, stirring continuously.
- Add the milk, a little at a time, stirring continuously.
- Cook till the mixture becomes thick and bubbly, stirring continuously.
- Stir in the cheese till melts completely.
- Add the roux into the simmering soup and cook till heat completely, stirring continuously.

Amount per serving 32

Timing Information:

Preparation	15 m
Cooking	30 m
Total Time	45 m

Nutritional Information:

Calories	171 kcal
Fat	7.4 g
Carbohydrates	21.2g
Protein	6.4 g
Cholesterol	21 mg
Sodium	810 mg

* Percent Daily Values are based on a 2,000 calorie diet.

Grocery Store Rotisserie Chowder

Ingredients

- 1/2 C. butter
- 1 small carrot, finely diced
- 1 stalk celery, diced
- 1 small onion, finely diced
- 1 clove garlic, minced
- 1/2 C. all-purpose flour
- 1 1/2 C. white corn kernels
- 1 1/2 C. yellow corn kernels
- 4 russet potatoes, diced
- 2 cooked rotisserie chicken breast halves, shredded
- 4 C. chicken stock, divided
- 2 1/2 C. half-and-half
- 1 pinch nutmeg
- Salt and ground black pepper to taste

Directions

- In a large pan, melt the butter on medium heat and sauté the carrot, celery, onion and garlic for about 2 minutes.
- Stir in the flour and cook for about 5 minutes, stirring continuously.

- Remove from the heat and keep aside to cool for about 15 minutes.
- In a large pan, mix together the corn kernels, potatoes, chicken, and 3 C. of the chicken stock on medium heat.
- Add remaining 1 C. of the chicken stock into the flour mixture and beat till well combined.
- Add the flour mixture into the pan with the corn mixture and bring to a gentle boil, stirring continuously.
- Boil for about 5 minutes, stirring continuously.
- Stir in the half-and-half, nutmeg, salt and black pepper and bring to a boil.
- Reduce the heat to low and simmer for about 20 minutes.

Amount per serving 8

Timing Information:

Preparation	25 m
Cooking	30 m
Total Time	1 h 10 m

Nutritional Information:

Calories	443 kcal
Fat	22 g
Carbohydrates	49.9g
Protein	15.2 g
Cholesterol	77 mg
Sodium	489 mg

* Percent Daily Values are based on a 2,000 calorie diet.

Condensed Cream Cheese Chowder

Ingredients

- 1 (14.75 oz.) can cream-style corn
- 1 (10.75 oz.) can condensed cream of potato soup
- 1 1/2 C. half-and-half cream
- 1/4 C. bacon bits, optional
- 2 green onion, chopped
- 1/4 tsp cayenne pepper
- 1 (8 oz.) package cold cream cheese, cubed
- 1 (4 oz.) can small shrimp, drained

Directions

- In a pan, mix together the cream-style corn, cream of potato soup, half-and-half, bacon bits, green onion on and cayenne pepper medium-high heat and bring to a boil.
- Stir in the cream cheese till melts completely.
- Stir in the shrimp and cook for about 1-2 minutes.

Amount per serving 6

Timing Information:

Preparation	10 m
Cooking	10 m
Total Time	20 m

Nutritional Information:

Calories	336 kcal
Fat	22.5 g
Carbohydrates	22.7g
Protein	13 g
Cholesterol	101 mg
Sodium	834 mg

* Percent Daily Values are based on a 2,000 calorie diet.

Milanese Chowder

Ingredients

- 2 tbsp butter
- 1 onion, chopped
- 2 cloves garlic, minced
- 1 red bell pepper, chopped
- 1 green bell pepper, chopped
- 2 C. chicken broth
- 1 lb. red potatoes cut into chunks
- 1/4 tsp ground white pepper
- 1/4 tsp ground cumin
- 3 1/2 C. whole kernel corn
- 4 oz. kielbasa, halved and sliced, optional
- 1/3 C. milk
- 1/3 C. heavy cream

Directions

- In a large pan, melt the butter on medium heat and cook the onion, garlic and bell peppers for about 10-15 minutes.
- Stir in the broth, potatoes, pepper and cumin and bring to a boil.
- Reduce the heat and simmer for about 20 minutes.
- In a blender, add half of the corn and pulse till smooth.

- Add the pureed corn, remaining whole corn, kielbasa, milk and cream in the simmering soup. And simmer for about 20 minutes.

Amount per serving 6

Timing Information:

Preparation	10 m
Cooking	50 m
Total Time	1 h

Nutritional Information:

Calories	322 kcal
Fat	15.5 g
Carbohydrates	42.8g
Protein	8 g
Cholesterol	42 mg
Sodium	213 mg

* Percent Daily Values are based on a 2,000 calorie diet.

60-Minute Corn Chowder

Ingredients

- 4 slices bacon, diced
- 1 onion, chopped
- 1 (14.75 oz.) can cream-style corn
- 1 1/2 C. cubed potatoes
- 1 (10.75 oz.) can condensed cream of mushroom soup
- 3 C. milk
- Salt and pepper to taste

Directions

- In a large saucepan, add the bacon and onions on medium heat and sauté for about 7 minutes.
- Add the corn, potatoes, soup, milk, salt and pepper and stir to combine.
- Increase the heat to high and bring to a boil.
- Reduce the heat to low and simmer, covered for about 25-35 minutes, stirring occasionally.

Amount per serving 3

Timing Information:

Preparation	10m
Cooking	50m
Total Time	1h

Nutritional Information:

Calories	553 kcal
Fat	28.3 g
Carbohydrates	60.4g
Protein	18.4 g
Cholesterol	45 mg
Sodium	1465 mg

* Percent Daily Values are based on a 2,000 calorie diet.

South Carolina Catfish Inspired Chowder

Ingredients

- 2 tbsp butter
- 1/2 small onion, chopped
- 1 (14 oz.) can chicken broth
- 1 C. water
- 1/2 C. chopped celery
- 1 C. sliced baby carrots
- 2 medium potatoes, cubed
- 3 C. milk, divided
- 1/3 C. cake flour
- 1 tsp celery salt
- 1 tsp salt
- 1/2 tsp ground black pepper
- 1 1/2 lb. catfish fillets cut into 1 inch pieces
- 1 1/2 C. shredded Cheddar cheese

Directions

- In a Dutch oven, melt the butter on medium heat and sauté the onion till tender.

- Stir in the chicken broth, water, celery, carrots and potatoes and cook for about 10 minutes, stirring occasionally.
- In a small bowl, add 1 1/2 C. of the milk and cake flour and beat till well combined.
- Add the flour mixture into the Dutch oven and stir to combine.
- Stir in the remaining milk, celery salt and pepper and cook for about 10 minutes, stirring occasionally.
- Stir in the catfish and cook for about 5 minutes.
- Stir in the Cheddar cheese and cook for about 5 minutes, stirring continuously.

Amount per serving 8

Timing Information:

Preparation	15 m
Cooking	30 m
Total Time	45 m

Nutritional Information:

Calories	347 kcal
Fat	18.5 g
Carbohydrates	20.9g
Protein	23.6 g
Cholesterol	78 mg
Sodium	968 mg

* Percent Daily Values are based on a 2,000 calorie diet.

Utica Inspired Chowder

Ingredients

- 2 1/2 lb. halibut steaks, cubed
- 1 red bell pepper, chopped
- 1 onion, chopped
- 3 stalks celery, chopped
- 3 cloves garlic, minced
- 1/4 C. olive oil
- 1 C. tomato juice
- 1/2 C. apple juice
- 2 (16 oz.) cans whole peeled tomatoes, mashed
- 2 tbsp chopped fresh parsley
- 1/2 tsp salt
- 1/2 tsp dried basil
- 1/8 tsp dried thyme
- 1/8 tsp ground black pepper

Directions

- In a large pan, heat the oil and sauté the peppers, celery, onion and garlic till tender.
- Add the tomato juice, apple juice, mashed tomatoes and herbs and simmer for about 30 minutes.
- Stir in the halibut pieces and simmer for about 30 minutes.

- Stir in the salt and pepper and remove from the heat.

Amount per serving 8

Timing Information:

Preparation	20 m
Cooking	1 h 10 m
Total Time	1 h 30 m

Nutritional Information:

Calories	262 kcal
Fat	10.3 g
Carbohydrates	10.7g
Protein	31.2 g
Cholesterol	45 mg
Sodium	400 mg

* Percent Daily Values are based on a 2,000 calorie diet.

How to Make a Fresh Corn Chowder

Ingredients

- 4 ears corn, kernels cut from cob
- 2 tbsp olive oil, divided
- 1 onion, diced
- 1 C. shredded carrot
- 1 stalk celery, chopped
- 1 clove garlic
- 4 C. chicken broth
- 4 red potatoes cut into bite-size pieces
- 2 C. light cream
- 1 (15 oz.) can cream-style corn
- 1 tsp finely chopped parsley
- Salt and ground black pepper to taste

Roux:

- 3 tbsp butter
- 2 tbsp all-purpose flour

Directions

- Set your oven to 350 degrees F before doing anything else.

- In a baking dish, mix together the corn kernels and 1 tbsp of the olive oil.
- Cook in the oven for about 20 minutes.
- In a large pan, heat 1 tbsp of the olive oil on medium heat and sauté the onion, carrot, celery and garlic for about 5-7 minutes.
- Stir in the chicken broth, roasted corn, potatoes, light cream, cream-style corn, parsley, salt and pepper and bring to a boil.
- In a small skillet, melt the butter on medium-low heat.
- Add the flour and cook for about 5 minutes, stirring continuously.
- Add the roux into the chowder and cooking for about 30 minutes, stirring occasionally.

Amount per serving 8

Timing Information:

Preparation	20 m
Cooking	1 h
Total Time	1 h 20 m

Nutritional Information:

Calories	313 kcal
Fat	20.4 g
Carbohydrates	30.9g
Protein	5.7 g
Cholesterol	54 mg
Sodium	729 mg

* Percent Daily Values are based on a 2,000 calorie diet.

Chowder 101

Ingredients

- 3 tbsp butter
- 1 onion, chopped
- 1 large potato, peeled and diced
- 1 bay leaf
- 1/2 tsp cumin
- 1/4 tsp dried sage
- 3 tbsp all-purpose flour
- 2 C. chicken stock
- 1 1/2 C. milk
- 1 1/2 C. frozen corn kernels
- 2 tbsp chopped parsley
- 2 tbsp chopped fresh chives
- 1/4 C. dry white wine
- 2 C. shredded Cheddar cheese
- Salt and pepper to taste

Directions

- In a large pan, melt the butter on medium high heat and sauté the onion, potato, bay leaf, cumin and sage for about 5 minutes.
- Add the flour and stir to coat well.

- Add the chicken stock and milk and bring to a boil, beating continuously.
- Reduce the heat and simmer for about 30 minutes, stirring occasionally.
- Stir in the corn, parsley, chives and wine and simmer for about 5 minutes.
- Discard the bay leaf and stir in the Cheddar cheese till melted completely.
- Stir in the salt and pepper and remove from the heat.

Amount per serving 6

Timing Information:

Preparation	15 m
Cooking	45 m
Total Time	1 h

Nutritional Information:

Calories	348 kcal
Fat	19.9 g
Carbohydrates	27.8g
Protein	14.7 g
Cholesterol	60 mg
Sodium	372 mg

* Percent Daily Values are based on a 2,000 calorie diet.

Country Roasted Chicken and Broccoli Chowder

Ingredients

- 4 slices turkey bacon, chopped
- 1 tbsp olive oil
- 2 cloves garlic, minced
- 1 onion, diced
- 2 carrots, chopped
- 2 stalks celery, chopped
- 1/2 C. all-purpose flour
- 1 (48 fluid oz.) can chicken broth
- 1 tsp ground cumin
- 1 tsp red pepper flakes
- 2 tsp garlic and herb seasoning blend
- 2 bay leaves
- 1/2 tsp ground thyme
- 1 tsp salt
- 1/2 tsp poultry seasoning
- 1 small head broccoli, cut into florets
- 1 1/2 C. half-and-half
- 1 potato, cubed
- 2 (6.5 oz.) cans chopped clams
- 1/2 lb. roasted chicken thigh meat, diced

- 1/4 C. butter, cubed
- 1 C. coarsely shredded smoked cheddar cheese

Directions

- In a large pan, heat the olive oil on medium heat and cook the bacon till browned.
- With a slotted spoon, transfer the bacon onto a paper towel lined plate to drain.
- In the same pan, add the garlic, onion, carrots and celery and cook for about 10 minutes.
- Stir in the flour and cook for about 10 minutes, stirring continuously.
- Add the chicken broth, cumin, red pepper flakes, garlic and herb seasoning blend, bay leaf, thyme, salt and poultry seasoning and bring to a boil on high heat.
- Reduce the heat to medium-low and simmer for about 10 minutes, stirring occasionally.
- Meanwhile, arrange a steamer basket over 1-inch of boiling water.
- Place the broccoli in steamer basket and cook, covered for about 2-4 minutes.
- Drain the broccoli and transfer into a blender.
- Add some of the half-and-half and pulse till smooth.
- Add the broccoli puree, remaining half-and-half, potato, clams, and chicken into the simmering chowder and bring to a simmer.

- Simmer for about 15 minutes.
- Add the cubed butter and stir till melted completely.
- Serve with a sprinkling of the Cheddar cheese.

Amount per serving 12

Timing Information:

Preparation	45 m
Cooking	55 m
Total Time	1 h 40 m

Nutritional Information:

Calories	317 kcal
Fat	19.9 g
Carbohydrates	14.7g
Protein	19.4 g
Cholesterol	79 mg
Sodium	1011 mg

* Percent Daily Values are based on a 2,000 calorie diet.

Caribbean Conch and Corn Chowder

Ingredients

- 1 lb. conch meat
- 1/4 C. margarine, divided
- 2 green onions, chopped
- 1 carrot, diced
- 1 stalk celery, diced
- 1 small sweet potato, peeled and diced
- 1 small red bell pepper, diced
- 1/2 C. fresh corn kernels
- 2 tbsp all-purpose flour
- 1 quart half-and-half
- 1 (14 oz.) can unsweetened coconut milk
- 2 C. fish stock
- 1 1/2 tbsp grated fresh ginger root
- Salt and pepper to taste
- 1 1/2 tsp hot sauce
- 1 bunch fresh cilantro, chopped

Directions

- In a pan, add the conch meat and enough water to cover and bring to a boil.
- Cook for about 15 minutes.
- Drain the conch meat ell.
- In a food processor, add the conch meat pulse till chopped finely.
- In a skillet, melt 2 tbsp of the margarine on medium heat and sauté the green onions, carrot, celery, sweet potato, red pepper and corn for about 5 minutes.
- In a large pan, melt remaining 2 tbsp of the margarine.
- Add the flour and cook till a roux is formed, stirring contentiously.
- Stir in the half-and-half, coconut milk, fish stock, ginger, salt, pepper, conch meat and vegetables and bring to a boil.
- Reduce the heat to low and simmer for about 15 minutes.
- Stir in the hot sauce and cilantro and simmer for about 15 minutes.

Amount per serving 8

Timing Information:

Preparation	20 m
Cooking	45 m
Total Time	1 h 5 m

Nutritional Information:

Calories	430 kcal
Fat	30.7 g
Carbohydrates	20g
Protein	20.5 g
Cholesterol	81 mg
Sodium	474 mg

* Percent Daily Values are based on a 2,000 calorie diet.

SASKATCHEWAN COUNTRY CHOWDER

Ingredients

- 1 lb. turkey bacon
- 2 carrots, diced
- 4 stalks celery, chopped
- 1 bay leaf
- 2 tbsp butter
- 2 tbsp all-purpose flour
- 4 C. milk
- 3 large potatoes, diced
- 1 (19 oz.) can corn, drained
- 1 pinch paprika

Directions

- Heat a large skillet on medium heat and cook the bacon for about 5 minutes.
- Transfer the bacon onto a paper towel lined plate to drain and then crumble it.
- Remove about half of the bacon grease from the skillet.
- In the remaining bacon grease, sauté the carrots, celery and bay leaf for about 5 minutes.
- In a large pan, melt the butter on medium-low heat.
- Stir in the flour.

- Slowly, stir in the milk and bring to a gentle boil.
- Cook for about 5 minutes, beating continuously.
- Stir in the crumbled bacon, potatoes, corn, paprika and carrot mixture and simmer for about 15 minutes, stirring occasionally.

Amount per serving 6

Timing Information:

Preparation	15 m
Cooking	30 m
Total Time	45 m

Nutritional Information:

Calories	489 kcal
Fat	18.6 g
Carbohydrates	62.3g
Protein	21.4 g
Cholesterol	51 mg
Sodium	984 mg

* Percent Daily Values are based on a 2,000 calorie diet.

How to Make a Can of Chowder

Ingredients

- 1 (10.75 oz.) can New England clam chowder
- 1 (10.75 oz.) can condensed cream of potato soup
- 1 (10.75 oz.) can condensed cream of celery soup
- 1 (6.5 oz.) can minced clams
- 1/2 C. chopped onion
- 1/2 C. chopped celery
- 1 tbsp margarine
- 4 C. half-and-half cream

Directions

- In a large pan, melt the margarine on and sauté the onion and celery till tender.
- Stir in the clam chowder, cream of potato soup, cream of celery soup, clams and half-and-half and cook till heated completely.

Amount per serving 6

Timing Information:

Preparation	10 m
Cooking	20 m
Total Time	30 m

Nutritional Information:

Calories	412 kcal
Fat	26 g
Carbohydrates	27.1g
Protein	17.6 g
Cholesterol	95 mg
Sodium	1198 mg

* Percent Daily Values are based on a 2,000 calorie diet.

Saturday's Dinner

Ingredients

- 1 tbsp olive oil
- 1 red onion, diced
- 3 cloves garlic, minced
- 1 red bell pepper, diced
- 3 potatoes, diced
- 3 carrots, diced
- 2 quarts chicken broth
- 1 lb. skinless, boneless chicken breast halves - chopped
- 1 (1 oz.) package ranch dressing mix
- 1 tsp crushed red pepper flakes
- Salt to taste
- Ground black pepper to taste
- 1/2 lb. processed cheese food, shredded
- 1 (16 oz.) package frozen green beans
- 1/4 C. butter
- 1/4 C. all-purpose flour

Directions

- In a large pan, heat the oil on medium heat and sauté the onion, garlic and red bell pepper till tender.

- Stir in the potatoes, carrots and chicken broth and bring to a boil.
- Reduce the heat to low and simmer for about 20 minutes.
- Stir in the chicken, ranch dressing mix, crushed red pepper, salt and pepper.
- Add the processed cheese and stir till melts completely.
- Stir in the green beans just before making the roux.
- In a skillet, melt the butter on medium heat.
- Stir in the flour and cook till a thick, golden brown roux is formed, stirring continuously.
- Add the roux into the soup and cook for about 5 minutes, stirring continuously.

Amount per serving 6

Timing Information:

Preparation	20 m
Cooking	40 m
Total Time	1 h

Nutritional Information:

Calories	459 kcal
Fat	21.4 g
Carbohydrates	40g
Protein	26.3 g
Cholesterol	90 mg
Sodium	925 mg

* Percent Daily Values are based on a 2,000 calorie diet.

VEGGIE SAMPLER CHOWDER

Ingredients

- 3 tbsp margarine
- 1 onion, finely diced
- 3 potatoes, peeled and diced
- 3/4 C. chopped celery
- 2 C. sliced carrots
- 2 tsp salt
- 1/8 tsp ground black pepper
- 3 C. chicken broth
- 3 C. milk
- 1/2 tsp dried parsley
- 1/4 C. cold water
- 1/4 C. cornstarch

Directions

- In a large pan, melt the butter on medium heat and sauté the onion till tender.
- Stir in the carrots and celery and cook for about 10 minutes.
- Add the broth, potatoes, salt and pepper and bring to a boil.
- Simmer for about 15-20 minutes.

- Stir in the milk and parsley and bring to a boil.
- In a bowl, dissolve the cornstarch into cold water.
- Add the cornstarch mixture into the hot soup and cook till well combined, stirring continuously.
- Serve immediately.

Amount per serving 7

Timing Information:

Preparation	20 m
Cooking	35 m
Total Time	55 m

Nutritional Information:

Calories	203 kcal
Fat	6.8 g
Carbohydrates	30.3g
Protein	6 g
Cholesterol	8 mg
Sodium	802 mg

* Percent Daily Values are based on a 2,000 calorie diet.

Rust Belt Chowder

Ingredients

- 1/4 C. butter, melted
- 1/4 C. chopped onion
- 1/4 C. all-purpose flour
- 4 C. milk
- 2 (15 oz.) cans creamed corn
- 1 1/2 C. shredded American cheese
- 1 tsp salt
- 1/4 tsp white pepper

Directions

- In a large pan, melt the butter on medium heat and sauté the onion till tender.
- Stir in the flour and cook till a paste like mixture is formed, stirring continuously.
- Add the milk and stir till the mixture becomes thick.
- Stir in the corn, cheese, salt and pepper and cook till the cheese is melted completely.
- Serve hot.

Amount per serving 6

Timing Information:

Preparation	20 m
Cooking	35 m
Total Time	55 m

Nutritional Information:

Calories	397 kcal
Fat	20.6 g
Carbohydrates	41.9g
Protein	14.9 g
Cholesterol	63 mg
Sodium	1407 mg

* Percent Daily Values are based on a 2,000 calorie diet.

Providence Inspired Chuckle Chowder

Ingredients

- 1 lb. shucked clams
- 3 C. clam juice
- 3 C. chicken stock
- 1/4 C. butter
- 2 onions, diced
- 2 large stalks celery, chopped, with leaves
- 1 (15 oz.) can fingerling potatoes, drained and quartered
- 3 tbsp dried dill weed
- 2 tbsp ground black pepper
- 1 tsp salt
- 1 pinch cayenne pepper
- 2 drops hot pepper sauce
- 1/4 C. chopped fresh parsley

Directions

- In a large pan, add the shucked clams, clam juice and chicken stock on medium-high heat and bring to a boil.
- Reduce the heat to medium-low and simmer for about 15 minutes.

- Meanwhile in a large skillet, melt the butter on medium heat and sauté the onion and celery till tender.
- Add the onion mixture, potatoes, dill, black pepper, salt, cayenne pepper and hot pepper sauce and simmer for about 15 minutes.
- Serve with a sprinkling of the parsley.

Amount per serving 4

Timing Information:

Preparation	20 m
Cooking	35 m
Total Time	55 m

Nutritional Information:

Calories	326 kcal
Fat	13.7 g
Carbohydrates	33.4g
Protein	19.7 g
Cholesterol	75 mg
Sodium	1899 mg

* Percent Daily Values are based on a 2,000 calorie diet.

CHOPPED CHOWDER

Ingredients

- 2 C. water
- 2 C. peeled and cubed potatoes
- 1/2 C. chopped onion
- 2 cloves garlic, chopped
- Salt and ground black pepper to taste
- 1/4 C. butter
- 1/4 C. all-purpose flour
- 2 C. 1% milk
- 1 (8 oz.) package low-fat cream cheese
- 1 C. shredded sharp Cheddar cheese
- 1 (15 oz.) can corn
- 1 1/2 C. cubed fully cooked chicken

Directions

- In a large pan, add the water, potatoes, onion, garlic, salt and pepper and bring to a boil.
- Reduce the heat and simmer, covered for about 8-10 minutes.
- Remove from the heat.
- In another large pan, melt the butter on medium heat.

- Stir in the flour and cook till smooth, stirring continuously.
- Slowly, stir in the milk and bring to a boil.
- Reduce the heat and simmer for about 2 minutes, stirring continuously.
- Add the cream cheese and Cheddar cheese and stir till melts completely.
- Add the potato mixture, corn and chicken into the cheese mixture and cook for about 10-15 minutes, stirring occasionally.

Amount per serving 6

Timing Information:

Preparation	30 m
Cooking	20 m
Total Time	50 m

Nutritional Information:

Calories	471 kcal
Fat	28.4 g
Carbohydrates	34.7g
Protein	21.5 g
Cholesterol	83 mg
Sodium	975 mg

* Percent Daily Values are based on a 2,000 calorie diet.

San Pedro Pepper Jack Chowder

Ingredients

- 3 Poblano peppers
- 1/4 C. butter
- 1/4 C. all-purpose flour
- 2 (32 oz.) cartons chicken broth
- 2 C. diced roasted chicken breast
- 2 (11 oz.) cans whole kernel corn with peppers
- 2 (15 oz.) cans black beans
- 2 C. shredded sharp Cheddar cheese
- 1 C. shredded pepper jack cheese
- 2 tbsp ground cumin
- 2 tsp garlic powder
- Salt and pepper to taste
- 2 C. tortilla chips, for topping

Directions

- Set the broiler of your oven and arrange oven rack about 6-inch from the heating element.
- Line a baking sheet with a piece of the foil.
- Cut the peppers in half from top to bottom and remove the stem, seeds and ribs.

- Arrange the peppers onto the prepared baking sheet, cut-side-down.
- Cook under the broiler for about 5 minutes.
- Place the blackened peppers into a bowl and with plastic wrap, seal tightly.
- Keep aside for about 20 minutes.
- After cooling, remove the skins of the peppers and then, chop them.
- Meanwhile in a pan, melt the butter on medium heat.
- Add the flour and cook for about 5 minutes, stirring continuously.
- Slowly, add the chicken broth, beating continuously.
- Bring to a gentle boil on medium heat and cook for about 10 minutes.
  - Stir in the diced peppers, diced chicken, corn, black beans, Cheddar cheese, pepper jack cheese, cumin, garlic powder, salt and pepper and bring to a simmer.
  - Simmer for about 10 minutes, stirring occasionally.
  - Serve with a sprinkling of the tortilla chips.

Amount per serving 8

Timing Information:

Preparation	15 m
Cooking	30 m
Total Time	1 h

Nutritional Information:

Calories	427 kcal
Fat	26 g
Carbohydrates	25.4g
Protein	24.7 g
Cholesterol	94 mg
Sodium	1710 mg

* Percent Daily Values are based on a 2,000 calorie diet.

Georgia Mixed Veggie Chowder

Ingredients

- 1 (16 oz.) package mixed frozen vegetables (broccoli, corn, red pepper)
- 2 tbsp butter
- 3/4 C. chopped onion
- 1 clove garlic, minced
- 1 (4 oz.) package sliced fresh mushrooms
- 1 tbsp Cajun seasoning
- 2 tbsp all-purpose flour
- 1 1/2 C. milk
- 1 lb. scallops - rinsed, drained, and cut in half
- 1 tsp salt
- 1/8 tsp ground black pepper

Directions

- In a pan, add the mixed vegetables and enough water to cover and bring to a boil.
- Boil for about 5 minutes.
- Drain the vegetables well and keep aside.
- In a large pan, melt the butter on medium-low heat and sauté the onion, garlic, mushrooms and Cajun seasoning for about 5 minutes.

- Stir in the flour and cook till well combined, stirring continuously.
- Add the milk and cook till the mixture becomes thick, stirring continuously.
- Add the scallops, salt, and pepper and cook for about 5-7 minutes.
- Stir in the vegetables and cook for about 2-3 minutes.
- Serve immediately.

Amount per serving 4

Timing Information:

Preparation	10 m
Cooking	20 m
Total Time	30 m

Nutritional Information:

Calories	355 kcal
Fat	9.5 g
Carbohydrates	32.7g
Protein	37.1 g
Cholesterol	91 mg
Sodium	1398 mg

* Percent Daily Values are based on a 2,000 calorie diet.

Classic Canadian Chowder

Ingredients

- 2 tbsp margarine
- 1 onion, chopped
- 2 stalks celery, chopped
- 2 carrots, chopped
- 1 1/2 C. uncooked wild rice
- 8 C. chicken stock
- 1 bay leaf
- 1/2 C. heavy cream
- 1 C. boneless chicken breast half, cooked and diced
- Salt and pepper to taste

Directions

- In a large pan, melt the margarine on medium heat and sauté the onion, celery and carrots for about 5-10 minutes.
- Add the rice and gently, stir to coat.
- Stir in the chicken stock and bay leaf.
  - Reduce the heat to low and simmer for about 1 hour, stirring occasionally.
- Stir in the heavy cream and remove from the heat.

- In a food processor, add 2 C. of the soup and pulse till smooth.
- Return the soup to the pan and stir in the chicken.
- Cook till heated completely.
- Stir in the salt and black pepper and remove from the heat.

Amount per serving 7

Timing Information:

Preparation	10 m
Cooking	1 h
Total Time	1 h 10 m

Nutritional Information:

Calories	274 kcal
Fat	12 g
Carbohydrates	31.2g
Protein	12 g
Cholesterol	39 mg
Sodium	864 mg

* Percent Daily Values are based on a 2,000 calorie diet.

Southern Parisian Chowder

Ingredients

- 2 tbsp olive oil
- 1 C. coarsely chopped onion
- 1/2 C. diced celery
- 3/4 C. chopped green bell pepper
- 3/4 C. chopped red bell pepper
- 2 cloves garlic, minced
- 1/2 tsp cayenne pepper
- 1 lb. andouille sausage, diced, optional
- 3 C. frozen corn kernels, thawed
- 2 bay leaves
- 2 tsp dried thyme
- 6 C. low-sodium chicken broth
- 3 Yukon Gold potatoes cut into 1/2-inch cubes
- 1 C. heavy cream
- Salt and ground black pepper to taste
- 1/2 C. chopped cilantro

Directions

- In a large pan, heat the olive oil on medium-high heat and sauté the onion, celery, bell peppers for about 5 minutes.

- Stir in the garlic, cayenne pepper, and diced andouille sausage and cook for about 1-2 minutes.
- Stir in the corn kernels, bay leaves and thyme and simmer for about 1 minute.
- Add the chicken broth and bring to a boil.
- Reduce the heat to medium-low and simmer for about 30 minutes, stirring occasionally.
- Stir in the potatoes and heavy cream and simmer, covered for about 20 minutes.
- Stir in the salt and black pepper and remove from the heat.
- Discard the bay leaves.
- Serve with a garnishing of the cilantro.

Amount per serving 8

Timing Information:

Preparation	20 m
Cooking	1 h
Total Time	1 h 20 m

Nutritional Information:

Calories	439 kcal
Fat	31.7 g
Carbohydrates	28.2g
Protein	13.3 g
Cholesterol	77 mg
Sodium	627 mg

* Percent Daily Values are based on a 2,000 calorie diet.

November's Chowder

Ingredients

- 2 C. peeled and diced potatoes
- 2 C. frozen mixed vegetables
- 1/4 C. chopped onion
- 1/4 C. finely chopped celery
- 1 tsp chopped fresh parsley
- 2 C. Swanson(R) Chicken Broth
- 1 1/2 C. diced cooked turkey
- 1/2 tsp poultry seasoning
- 1/4 C. all-purpose flour
- 1 1/2 C. fat free half-and-half
- 1/2 tsp sriracha chili garlic sauce
- Salt and pepper to taste
- 2 slices bacon, cooked and crumbled

Directions

- In a large pan, add the potatoes, mixed vegetables, onions, celery, parsley and broth on medium heat and bring to a boil.
- Reduce the heat and simmer, covered for about 10 minutes.
- Stir in turkey and poultry seasoning.

- Add the flour and the half-and-half and cook till smooth, stirring continuously.
- Cook till the mixture becomes slightly thick, stirring gently.
- Stir in the sriracha sauce, salt and pepper and remove from the heat.
- Serve hot with a garnishing of the crumbled bacon.

Amount per serving 4

Timing Information:

Preparation	15 m
Cooking	20 m
Total Time	35 m

Nutritional Information:

Calories	319 kcal
Fat	6.6 g
Carbohydrates	40.7g
Protein	25.2 g
Cholesterol	52 mg
Sodium	870 mg

* Percent Daily Values are based on a 2,000 calorie diet.

STATEN ISLAND INSPIRED CHOWDER

Ingredients

- 1 pint shucked clams
- 1 C. tomato and clam juice cocktail
- 2 potatoes, cleaned and chopped
- 1 C. chopped green bell pepper
- 1/4 C. chopped green onions
- 1/4 tsp ground black pepper
- 1 (14.5 oz.) can Italian-style diced tomatoes

Directions

- Chop the clams, reserving the juice.
- Strain the clam juice into a bowl to remove bits of shell.
- In the bowl of clam juice, add enough water to equal 1 1/2 C. of the liquid.
- In a large pan, add the clam juice mixture, clam-tomato juice cocktail, potatoes, bell peppers, scallions and black pepper and bring to a boil.
- Reduce the heat and simmer, covered for about 15 minutes.
- Stir in the undrained tomatoes and chopped clams and cook till heated completely.

Amount per serving 8

Timing Information:

Preparation	20 m
Cooking	25 m
Total Time	45 m

Nutritional Information:

Calories	82 kcal
Fat	0.2 g
Carbohydrates	< 15.8g
Protein	3.9 g
Cholesterol	5 mg
Sodium	203 mg

* Percent Daily Values are based on a 2,000 calorie diet.

American Comfort Chowder

Ingredients

- 1 lb. turkey bacon, diced
- 3 onions, diced
- 1 bunch celery, diced
- 3 tbsp minced garlic
- 2 quarts water, divided
- 1 gallon heavy whipping cream
- 1 C. butter
- 1 3/4 C. all-purpose flour
- 18 potatoes, peeled and diced
- 2 (16 oz.) packages frozen corn
- 1 red bell pepper, diced
- 2 pinches of red pepper flakes
- 1 pinch salt and ground black pepper

Directions

- In a large heavy-bottom pan, add the bacon on medium-high heat and cook for about 10 minutes.
- Add the onions, celery and garlic and stir to combine.
- Add 1 quart of the water and cook, covered for about 5 minutes.

- Stir in the remaining 1 quart water and cream and reduce the heat to medium.
- In a pan, melt the butter on medium heat.
- Stir in the flour and cook till a paste is formed, stirring continuously.
- Stir in the potatoes and cook for about 5 minutes, stirring continuously.
- Slowly, add the potato mixture into cream mixture, stirring continuously.
- Cook for about 30-40 minutes.
- Heat a cast iron skillet on medium heat and cook the corn and red bell pepper for about 10-15 minutes.
- Add the corn mixture, red pepper flakes, salt, and pepper into the soup and serve.

Amount per serving 50

Timing Information:

Preparation	20 m
Cooking	1 h
Total Time	1 h 20 m

Nutritional Information:

Calories	408 kcal
Fat	33.4 g
Carbohydrates	23.9g
Protein	5.5 g
Cholesterol	117 mg
Sodium	143 mg

* Percent Daily Values are based on a 2,000 calorie diet.

2-Cheese Red Potato Chowder

Ingredients

- 5 small red potatoes cut into bite-size pieces
- 2 tbsp olive oil
- 1 onion, diced
- 2 stalks celery, thinly sliced
- 2 tbsp all-purpose flour
- 1/2 tsp salt
- 1/4 tsp ground black pepper
- 4 C. 2% milk
- 1 cooked salmon fillet, flaked
- 1 1/4 C. frozen peas
- 1 1/4 C. frozen corn
- 1 tsp dried dill weed
- 1/2 C. shredded reduced-fat Swiss cheese
- 1/2 C. shredded reduced-fat Cheddar cheese
- 1 green onion, finely chopped

Directions

- In a large pan of salted water, add the potatoes and bring to a boil.
- Reduce the heat to medium-low and simmer for about 20 minutes.

- Drain the potatoes well.
- In a large pan, heat the olive oil on medium-high heat and sauté the onion and celery for about 5-7 minutes.
- Add the flour, salt and pepper and stir till well combined.
- Slowly, add the milk and bring to a boil, stirring continuously.
- Reduce the heat to medium and simmer for about 10 minutes.
- Add the potatoes, flaked salmon, peas, corn, and dill and cook for about 10 minutes.
- Stir in the Swiss cheese and Cheddar cheese and cook for about 5 minutes.
- Serve hot with a garnishing of the green onion.

Amount per serving 6

Timing Information:

Preparation	15 m
Cooking	50 m
Total Time	1 h 5 m

Nutritional Information:

Calories	388 kcal
Fat	13.1 g
Carbohydrates	46.5g
Protein	22.8 g
Cholesterol	37 mg
Sodium	417 mg

* Percent Daily Values are based on a 2,000 calorie diet.

Leek Lunch Box Chowder

Ingredients

- 3 leeks
- 6 tbsp butter, divided
- 1/4 C. all-purpose flour
- 2 (15 oz.) cans chicken broth
- 5 small red potatoes, peeled and diced
- 2 slices crispy cooked bacon, chopped
- Salt and ground black pepper to taste
- 1/2 C. water as needed
- 1 C. half-and-half

Directions

- Cut the roots of the leeks and the tips of the leaves.
- Make a vertical cut from the root end to the tops, being careful to not cut through completely.
- Slice the leeks into quarter-inch strips.
- In a skillet, melt 1/2 of the butter on medium-high heat and sauté the leeks for about 3-5 minutes.
- Transfer the leeks into a slow cooker.
- In the same skillet, melt the remaining butter on low heat.
- Slowly, add the flour and cook till smooth, beating continuously.

- Slowly, add the chicken broth and cook till well combined, beating continuously.
- Place the broth mixture over the leek in the slow cooker.
- Add the bacon, potatoes, salt and pepper and stir to combine.
- Set the slow cooker on Low and cook, covered for about 2 hours.
- Stir in the half-and-half and cook for about 1 hour.

Amount per serving 6

Timing Information:

Preparation	10 m
Cooking	3 h 15 m
Total Time	3 h 25 m

Nutritional Information:

Calories	326 kcal
Fat	18.1 g
Carbohydrates	35.3g
Protein	7 g
Cholesterol	52 mg
Sodium	865 mg

* Percent Daily Values are based on a 2,000 calorie diet.

Sanibel Island Scallop Chowder

Ingredients

- 4 C. chicken broth
- 4 potatoes cut into cubes
- 1 (14 oz.) can whole kernel corn, drained
- 1 onion, chopped
- 1/4 C. flour
- 1 C. heavy whipping cream
- 1/2 lb. sea scallops
- 1/2 lb. peeled, deveined, and cooked shrimp
- 1/4 C. dry potato flakes
- 1/4 tsp garlic pepper
- 1 pinch salt

Directions

- In a slow cooker, mix together the broth, potatoes, corn, onion and flour.
- Set the slow cooker on Low and cook, covered for about 6 hours.
- Stir in the cream, scallops, shrimp, potato flakes and garlic pepper.
- Now, set the slow cooker on High and cook, covered for about 35-45 minutes.

- Season with the salt and serve.

Amount per serving 8

Timing Information:

Preparation	15 m
Cooking	6 h 35 m
Total Time	6 h 50 m

Nutritional Information:

Calories	339 kcal
Fat	14.6 g
Carbohydrates	38.4g
Protein	15.3 g
Cholesterol	112 mg
Sodium	849 mg

* Percent Daily Values are based on a 2,000 calorie diet.

Lemon Pepper Seafood Sampler Chowder

Ingredients

- 1/4 C. butter
- 3 tbsp minced garlic
- 1/3 C. flour
- 4 C. half-and-half
- 1 C. dry vegetable soup mix
- 1/2 C. dried onion flakes
- 2 tbsp lemon pepper
- 1 pinch dried thyme
- 1 pinch saffron
- 1 C. diced salmon
- 1 C. diced halibut
- 1 C. peeled and deveined shrimp
- 1 C. peeled and deveined prawns
- 1 C. scallops

Directions

- In a large pan, add the butter and garlic on medium-high heat and cook till the butter is melted.

- Stir in the flour and cook for about 1 minute, beating continuously.
- Slowly, add the half-and-half and cook till smooth, beating continuously.
- Add the vegetable soup mix, onion flakes, lemon pepper, thyme and saffron and cook for about 5-10 minutes, stirring occasionally.
- Stir in the salmon, halibut, shrimp, prawns and scallops and bring to a simmer.
- Reduce the heat to medium-low and simmer for about 30 minutes, stirring occasionally.

Amount per serving 8

Timing Information:

Preparation	20 m
Cooking	40 m
Total Time	1 h

Nutritional Information:

Calories	434 kcal
Fat	24.4 g
Carbohydrates	30.8g
Protein	23.9 g
Cholesterol	144 mg
Sodium	1499 mg

* Percent Daily Values are based on a 2,000 calorie diet.

THANKS FOR READING! JOIN THE CLUB AND KEEP ON COOKING WITH 6 MORE COOKBOOKS....

http://bit.ly/1TdrStv

To grab the box sets simply follow the link mentioned above, or tap one of book covers.

This will take you to a page where you can simply enter your email address and a PDF version of the box sets will be emailed to you.

Hope you are ready for some serious cooking!

http://bit.ly/1TdrStv

Come On...
Let's Be Friends :)

We adore our readers and love connecting with them socially.

Like BookSumo on Facebook and let's get social!

Facebook

And also check out the BookSumo Cooking Blog.

Food Lover Blog

Printed in Great
Britain
by Amazon